Designer DB Plus®

Designer DB Plus®

Game-Changing Tax Reduction & Retirement Strategy:

For Today's Small Business Owners

Unlocking Major Tax Deductions to Build Multimillion-Dollar Retirement Accounts in Under Ten Years for a Secure and Confident Business Exit

STEPHEN ARNOLD

COPYRIGHT © 2024

STEPHEN ARNOLD

All rights are reserved. No part of this book may be reproduced, distributed, or transmitted in any form or by any means, including photocopying, recording, or other electronic or mechanical methods, without the prior written permission of the author, except in the case of brief quotations embodied in critical reviews and certain other noncommercial uses permitted by copyright law. For permission requests, write to the author at the address provided in the acknowledgments section of this book.

Printed in the United States of America

First Printing Edition, 2024

I S B N 978-1-965360-18-7

Dedication

I would like to extend my sincere gratitude and recognition to the following individuals:

To Kathleen, my wife, co-author, and partner: Your talent and commitment to our work are deeply appreciated. Your unwavering dedication to this industry and to our clients is truly admirable. You take great pride in empowering clients with the knowledge and providing guidance for successful business exits and secure retirement. Your ability to help others through these crucial life transitions, coupled with your compassion and wisdom, is a constant source of inspiration.

To Zak Kenne, my esteemed partner and dear friend:

Your profound expertise as an Enrolled Actuary, coupled with your impressive array of professional designations, stands as a testament to your unwavering dedication to your craft. Your tireless commitment to studying, interpreting, understanding, and implementing complex actuarial concepts is nothing short of exceptional. Your passion and diligence have not only set a high standard in our field but have also delivered immense value to countless small business owners. Through your exceptional knowledge of Qualified plans, you have empowered many to confidently achieve their financial goals. Your remarkable contributions are deeply appreciated and continue to inspire all who have the privilege of working with you.

To Dean Zayed, Founder and CEO of Brookstone Capital Management, my dear friend and esteemed colleague. Your unwavering support and belief in our vision have been instrumental in bringing our plans and services to the Brookstone family. Through your guidance and leadership, we've had the privilege of reaching thousands of advisors, empowering them to serve their clients better and achieve new heights in their practices. Your dedication to excellence and your commitment to fostering a community of trust and collaboration have made all the difference. Thank you for being a true partner in every sense of the word.

To our administrative team: Your tireless efforts form the foundation of our operations. Your commitment to meeting our clients' needs with the highest level of professionalism allows us to focus on our core mission of making a meaningful impact in our clients' lives. Your contributions are invaluable and deeply appreciated.

As a cohesive team, we remain committed to making a lasting positive impact on the lives of those we serve, guiding them toward a future of promise and prosperity.

Disclaimer

This book provides a general overview of sophisticated retirement planning strategies and is intended for informational purposes only. The concepts presented, particularly the Designer DB Plus® plan, are complex and require specialized expertise to implement correctly.

Readers should not attempt to establish or administer these plans without guidance from qualified professionals. If you need expert assistance, please consult with appropriate professionals. Retirement Actuarial Services LLC does not give tax or investment advice.

Table of Contents

PREFACE ix
Chapter One: America's Retirement Planning Crisis 1
Chapter Two: Introduction to Retirement Plans 15
Chapter Three: Early 20th Century Defined Benefit Plan Problems 20
Chapter Four: Transition to Cash Balance Profit Share/ 401k Combination Plans 27
Chapter Five: 21st Century Retirement Planning Solution 39
Chapter Six: Why hasn't my tax advisor recommended this to me? 51
Chapter Seven: Additional Benefits of the Designer DB Plus® Plan 56
Chapter Eight: Key Dates for Proactive Tax Planning with a Custom Designer DB Plus® Plan 62

Foreword

In today's complex world of financial planning, securing a comfortable retirement is one of the biggest challenges we face. This is especially true for small business owners, who must balance running their business with planning for their future. This book, *"Designer DB Plus®: Game-Changing Tax Reduction & Retirement Strategy: For Today's Small Business Owners,"* is an essential resource for addressing these challenges.

Author Stephen Arnold brings decades of experience in financial services, specializing in qualified retirement plans, to create a book to educate and raise awareness among business owners about these robust plans. He introduces the Designer DB Plus® plan, which combines the best features of Cash Balance, Profit Sharing, 401(k), and 401(h) plans. This approach gives small business owners a powerful way to save on taxes, grow their retirement savings faster, and secure their financial future beyond what traditional retirement plans can offer.

This book stands out because it breaks down complex ideas into clear, actionable strategies. Arnold explains the limits of standard retirement plans and shows the significant benefits of the Designer DB Plus® plan. Each chapter builds a strong case for why small business owners should rethink their retirement planning approach.

The book's focus on proactive tax planning is particularly valuable. In today's world, where tax efficiency can greatly impact long-term wealth, the strategies in this book offer readers ways to save significantly on taxes while building their retirement funds. Real-world examples and detailed timelines for implementation make this guide practical and useful.

Arnold also addresses an often-overlooked aspect of retirement planning: post-retirement medical expenses. By including information on 401(h) accounts, he provides a more complete approach to retirement planning than most resources.

This book is a new way forward; it challenges common assumptions and provides a clear path to a more secure retirement. Whether you're a small business owner, financial advisor, or tax professional, this book is a must-read for anyone interested in advanced retirement planning strategies.

The ideas in this book can transform retirement outcomes for many entrepreneurs and small business owners. It's strongly recommended for anyone serious about maximizing their retirement savings and securing their financial future.

Preface

This book is intended to expand your understanding of tax reduction and retirement planning by exploring strategies and options beyond the traditional 401(k), SEP, Solo 401(k), and SIMPLE IRA plans. Through examples and explanations, we aim to provide you with valuable insights into alternative methods for optimizing your financial future. Whether you're seeking innovative tax-saving techniques or retirement planning strategies that go beyond the basics, this book will put you on the right path to seek assistance and determine if these more sophisticated plans suit your needs.

If you are a successful business owner looking to:

- Significantly reduce or zero out your state and federal taxes
- Make tax-deductible contributions to your retirement in the hundreds of thousands of dollars annually
- Creditor-protect your retirement savings from lawsuits and judgments
- Accelerate the growth of your retirement savings without aggressive investment risk
- Pay for the high cost of medical expenses in retirement with tax-free money
- Exit your business with a tax reduction strategy for the sale of your business
- Meet the new retirement employee mandates while controlling costs

- Tax deduct and save far more than 401(k)s, SEPs, and Simple plans' maximum limits
- Qualify for the elusive QBI 20% tax deduction in most cases

Then, a custom-designed Designer DB Plus® plan may be right for you.

Unlike big company executives, small business owners are disadvantaged regarding the resources, options, and education needed for proactive tax reduction and retirement planning.

Pension plans have been the cornerstone of financial planning for decades, favoring big companies and highly paid executives who retire with large lifetime pensions. Successful small business owners have been left in the dark regarding changes in legislation that have opened up flexible hybrid pension plans to millions of small business owners.

Most CPAs or tax advisors today have not been provided the education on the many changes to regulations in retirement tax savings strategies beyond cookie-cutter 401(k) plans, SEPs, and Simple IRAs that can be implemented for small business owners.

This leaves a massive gap in educating small business owners on plans that can be life-changing for them.

Further, the 401(k) and other basic retirement plans benefit the employees more than the owners because the owners cannot contribute and accumulate enough money to replace their income in retirement. The limit to a 401(k) with catch-up is not enough for high-income earners to safely collect the needed assets to retire with the same lifestyle throughout their retirement years.

Designer DB Plus® favors the owners with the lion's share of the tax-deductible contributions while still providing the required benefits to the employees to comply with nondiscrimination laws. Owners often average over 90% of the hundreds of thousands of dollars in tax-deductible contributions for themselves.

We at Retirement Actuarial Services LLC have taken years of experience and expertise in the field of advanced retirement planning and made it available for small business owners and their tax advisors to learn how these plans can profoundly impact their ability to reduce tax burdens while preparing themselves for a secure lifetime income with less investment risk by leveraging large tax-deductible contributions to the plan.

Proactive tax planning with a team of professionals specializing in designing and administering tax-deductible combination retirement plans can secure up to 80% of your working-year salary in retirement for the rest of your life.

In addition to the significant tax savings and accelerated retirement growth, a Designer DB Plus® plan offers unparalleled flexibility and control. You can tailor the plan to fit your specific business needs and financial goals, ensuring that your retirement strategy is as unique as your business. Making substantial contributions and receiving tax deductions provides a robust financial cushion, protecting your wealth from market volatility and ensuring steady growth.

These plans are designed to comply with all current regulations, providing peace of mind that your retirement savings strategy is legally sound and optimized for maximum benefit. With a well-crafted Designer DB Plus® plan, you can confidently navigate the complexities of retirement planning, knowing that your future is secure.

Retirement Actuarial Services LLC is dedicated to empowering small business owners with the knowledge and tools to make informed decisions about reducing their tax liabilities and maximizing their retirement planning. Our team is here to guide you through every step of the process, from initial plan design to ongoing administration and compliance. We understand your unique challenges and are committed to helping you achieve your retirement goals confidently and efficiently.

CHAPTER ONE

America's Retirement Planning Crisis

The United States faces a growing challenge in securing the retirement well-being of its workforce. Traditionally, many businesses haven't offered formal retirement plans, leaving employees to shoulder the responsibility of saving for their future on their own. This has created a potential future burden on social safety net programs.

A confluence of factors, including insufficient savings, limited access to robust retirement plans, and a knowledge gap regarding effective retirement strategies beyond the basic cookie-cutter 401k, SEP, Solo 401k, and Simple IRA, has created a concerning landscape.

States are now acting on this crisis and mandating that small business owners implement employee retirement plans or face penalties. Many business owners make the mistake of not knowing their options and defaulting to 401(k)s, SEP, Solo 401k, and Simple IRA Plans. These plans have limitations, such as:

- Low Maximum tax-deductible contributions for 2024:
  Simple IRA with a catch-up of $19,500
  401k with a Catch-up of $30,500
  SEP contributions of $69,000
  Solo 401k with a catch-up of $76,500
- Lack of investment choices for the participants.
- Burdensome questions for the owner from employees about their benefits and investments.

These plans may be suitable for some businesses, but many business owners, when properly educated about Cash Balance/Profit Share Defined Benefit Plans, would much rather have the benefits of:

- Large tax-deductible contributions in the hundreds of thousands annually, often with over 90% of the contribution going to the owner's benefit while still meeting compliance and nondiscrimination laws for employee benefits.
- Flexibility on annual contributions. In some years, when business is good, you may want to save and deduct more, and then a lower amount in another year.

This favors the business owner rather than limiting what they can save for themselves and not having to give too much of the contribution to the employees.

However, a powerful solution has emerged: hybrid retirement plans combining Cash Balance Defined Benefit structures with Profit Sharing and 401(k) options like Designer DB Plus® for business owners of all entities, including 1099 contractors and Sole Proprietors with or without employees. These plans offer a powerful advantage: the ability to make significant tax-deductible contributions, ranging from $75,000 to a staggering $1 million annually in some cases. This flexibility empowers small business owners to build a more secure and prosperous retirement future.

Building on this concept, the Designer DB Plus® plan from Retirement Actuarial Services is a sophisticated financial planning tool that integrates custom-designed combination plans in full compliance with IRS and Department of Labor regulations. This innovative approach is designed to maximize contribution potential while providing a flexible funding strategy for tax reduction and retirement planning, primarily benefiting business owners without neglecting the interests of their employees.

In practice, the business owner, who is also classified as an employee of their company, implements a plan that combines IRS-approved, tax-deductible retirement plans. This structure ensures full adherence to all applicable laws and regulations. While owners participate in all aspects of the combined plans, employee participation is limited to the Profit Share/401k component. This strategic arrangement allows owners to allocate a significantly higher proportion of tax-deductible contributions to the Cash Balance portion of the plan, from which employees are excluded. The 401k/profit share element addresses discrimination testing requirements and provides benefits for eligible employees.

Typically, this integrated approach results in over 90% of the total contribution being allocated to the owner while still offering substantial benefits to eligible employees. The integrity and compliance of our plans are ensured through certification by our Enrolled Actuary, recognized as an expert by both the IRS and the Department of Labor in this specialized area of financial planning. Furthermore, to ensure seamless operation, plan administration is managed by our dedicated administration services.

This comprehensive approach offers a powerful tool for business owners seeking to optimize their retirement planning and tax strategies while maintaining compliance and providing for their employees.

Now, let's look at the following case implemented for a software engineering firm with five employees. As you will see, in the following case, the owner contributed over 535,000 dollars in the first year, qualified for the elusive 20% QBI (Qualified Business Income Tax Deduction), and saved over 256,000 dollars in taxes and deferral. The QBI 20% Income tax deduction that he could not Qualify for before the Designer DB Plus® plan's implementation now qualified him to receive 65,992 dollars back in his pocket. And if that was not enough, a significant portion of the contribution was earmarked for tax-free health and medical expense reimbursement in retirement!

Additionally, this plan-controlled employee costs and complied with all regulations, giving the owner 94% of the tax-deductible contribution to his retirement while providing valuable benefits to keep and retain good employees.

Business Owner Opens Designer DB Plus®

CASE: Sunil is 43 years old, married, and the Owner of a thriving Software Engineering firm. Sunil has five employees, and they file as an S Corporation. As a result, he nets approximately $865,000 after expenses.

GOAL: Sunit wants to pay lower taxes, ensure he has Enough retirement savings to maintain his lifestyle and be prepared for the high cost of medical and health care in retirement.

SOLUTION: Designer DB Plus® cash balance PS/401k Combination Plan.

DEDUCTION: As an owner of a pass-through entity, it is crucial to reduce the Net Operating Income to qualify for the Qualified Business Income Deduction (Section 199A) for up to an additional 20% of his Qualified Business Income.

Designer DB Plus® Plan

Net profit after Expenses:	$865,000
Plan Contribution:	$535,040
Qualified Business Income:	$329,960
QBI Pass-through Deduction:	-$65,992
Taxable Income:	$263,968

Results: Percentage to Owner 94%
$502,937   Retirement Savings $502,937
$256.698 Tax Savings and Deferral*

*Tax savings and deferral compared to no Plan and (Section 199A) QBI deduction. The case assumes an estimated 37% tax rate. RAS does not provide tax advice. This example is based on specific assumptions and is used for illustrative purposes only.

Note: No matter how your business is structured or the type of business, as long as you are looking to reduce taxes and accelerate the amount accumulated for retirement, there is a plan that is right for you.

The Retirement Planning Challenge for Small Business Owners

The demands of running a successful small business can often overshadow the critical task of retirement planning. This can lead to several significant challenges for small business owners in securing their financial future. Relying on the sale of their business for retirement is also another common mistake. Many small businesses overestimate what they will sell for and the sales tax upon the sale.

1. **Insufficient Retirement Savings:** Many small business owners struggle to accumulate adequate retirement savings, which can potentially lead to financial vulnerability in their later years.

2. **Limited Access to Structured Retirement Plans:** Small businesses frequently lack formal retirement plans, leaving both owners and employees without a well-defined path for saving toward retirement.

3. **Delayed Planning Focus:** Entrepreneurs often prioritize business growth and investment over retirement planning, which can significantly reduce the time horizon for accumulating sufficient retirement funds.

4. **Knowledge Gap Regarding Enhanced Tax-Advantaged Options:** A lack of awareness exists concerning retirement plans with significantly higher tax-deductible contributions compared to traditional options like 401(k)s, SEPs, Solo 401K, and IRAs.

Policy Initiatives to Address the Challenge

In response to the growing concern regarding small business owners' retirement security, several U.S. states are taking proactive steps. These states have implemented or are in the process of implementing legislation that mandates employers to establish retirement savings plans for their employees.

Furthermore, the 2020 Secure Act recognized the importance of overcoming potential barriers to plan implementation. This landmark legislation introduced measures to reduce the financial burden on businesses associated with establishing retirement plans. These measures help offset the cost of design, documentation, and plan administration, making it easier for employers to provide this valuable benefit to their staff.

California's mandatory retirement plan legislation serves as a prime example of this growing trend. While such mandates aim to improve retirement security, there are potential challenges for business owners to consider.

One key concern is the implementation of this framework. Faced with new regulations, some business owners might default to the most readily available options, such as 401(k)s, SEPs, Solo 401k, and Simple IRAs. While these plans offer some benefits, they may not be the optimal solution for every business.

While meeting the legal requirements outlined in state mandates is essential, business owners have a significant opportunity to go beyond basic compliance. There are more sophisticated retirement savings plans available that, while requiring more complex calculations by a qualified professional (Enrolled Actuary and Third Party Administrator service provider), can offer substantial benefits.

These plans allow for significantly higher tax-deductible contributions compared to traditional options like 401(k)s, SEPs, Solo 401k, and Simple IRAs. This translates to a greater portion of the business owner's contribution being directed toward their retirement savings account and not the employees' accounts. Imagine a scenario where a business owner can achieve a tax deduction of, say, $200,000 to $400,000 annually and capture, on average, over 90% of the tax-deductible contribution for himself. These specialized plans enable a significant portion of these contributions to be allocated toward building a retirement nest egg that can potentially replace 80% of the owner's pre-retirement salary. This stands in stark contrast to the limitations of traditional plans, where contribution limits might be as low as $19,500 or maxed at $76,500 annually, depending on the plan. Such limitations can make it difficult for business owners to accumulate sufficient savings to achieve a secure retirement.

The limitations of traditional plans highlight the need for alternative strategies. Cash balance plans combined with profit-sharing elements offer a compelling solution for business owners seeking to maximize their retirement savings.

However, it's important to understand the regulatory landscape. These plans must comply with Department of Labor (DOL) and Internal Revenue Service (IRS) regulations to ensure nondiscrimination. This means including employees in the plan and allocating a calculated portion of the contributions toward them.

The key here lies in the design. By incorporating a Cash Balance plan and a 401k/profit-sharing plan, we can strategically direct a larger portion of the contributions toward the business owner's retirement savings. This optimized approach creates a hybrid plan that effectively addresses the limitations of traditional options.

Furthermore, these combination plans offer a significant benefit in terms of administrative efficiency. Compared to the labor-intensive management of traditional 401(k) plans, hybrid plans can streamline the retirement savings process for business owners, allowing them to focus on core business activities.

Addressing Challenges with Traditional 401(k) Plans

While traditional 401(k) plans offer some benefits for employee retirement savings, they can present limitations for business owners. The contribution limits for these plans may not be sufficient for business owners to accumulate the necessary funds for a secure retirement.

Furthermore, the administrative burden associated with managing traditional 401(k) plans can be significant. Employees often require guidance with investment decisions within the plan, which can be time-consuming for business owners to address.

The Advantages of Hybrid Retirement Plans

The hybrid retirement plans we discussed offer distinct advantages that address these challenges. These plans provide a crucial benefit for business owners: the ability to make significantly higher contributions toward their own retirement compared to traditional 401(k) plans. This allows them to accumulate a more substantial retirement nest egg.

For employees, participation in these plans is fully funded by the employer without individual participation by the employee, eliminating the need for individual investment decisions. The employer determines the contribution amount allocated on behalf of each employee to a pooled account with the help of a credible third-party administration firm, simplifying plan administration. This translates to a streamlined process for both the business owner and employees.

A Win-Win Solution

In essence, these hybrid plans offer a win-win scenario. Business owners gain the ability to save more effectively for their retirement, while employees automatically benefit from employer contributions. This not only enhances employee benefits but can also serve as a valuable retention tool, fostering a sense of loyalty within the workforce.

States with Mandatory or Planned Retirement Savings Programs (as of January 2024):

1. California: The Cal Savers program mandates that all employers with at least one employee facilitate a retirement savings plan. Phased deadlines for registration exist, with a target completion date of December 31, 2025.

2. Colorado: The Colorado Secure Savings program requires businesses that have been operational for at least two years and have five or more employees to facilitate a retirement savings plan.

3. Connecticut: My CT Savings mandates that employers with at least five employees facilitate participation in the state's retirement savings program.

4. Delaware: Businesses employing more than five staff members are required to participate in the DE EARNS program, which is scheduled for implementation by January 1, 2025.

5. Illinois: The Illinois Secure Choice program mandates that employers with five or more employees who do not currently offer a qualified retirement plan facilitate a retirement savings plan.

6. Maryland: Maryland mandates that employers offer a retirement savings option to their employees. This can be achieved through either a traditional pension plan or participation in the state-sponsored Maryland Saves program.

7. Massachusetts: The Massachusetts Defined Contribution CORE Plan is a targeted program designed for non-profit organizations with twenty or fewer employees. This plan offers both tax-deferred and post-tax contribution options, promoting retirement savings within this specific employer category.

8. New York: The New York State is currently developing its Secure Choice Savings Program (SCSP). This initiative suggests a forthcoming state mandate requiring employers to offer retirement savings plans.

9. Nevada: The Nevada Employee Savings Trust mandates that employers with more than five employees and a minimum of 36 months of operation must provide access to this program or a comparable qualified retirement plan.

10. Oregon: The Oregon Saves program mandates that all employers facilitate participation in the program if they do not currently offer a qualified retirement savings plan to their employees.

In recognition of the critical importance of retirement security, these aforementioned states have implemented proactive legislative measures. These initiatives aim to ensure that a greater number of employees have access to retirement savings plans. The specific program details, including deadlines and potential penalties for non-compliance, vary by state.

Consequently, employers need to familiarize themselves thoroughly with the regulations applicable to their specific state. This proactive approach will ensure compliance with state mandates and empower them to make informed decisions regarding their employees' retirement planning options.

Conclusion

Beyond simply complying with state mandates, selecting the most suitable retirement plan is crucial for any business owner. This decision necessitates a comprehensive understanding of the plan's features and its alignment with both the current and anticipated needs of the business.

Opting for an unsuitable plan can lead to significant financial repercussions. These repercussions can manifest as excessive costs for the business and potentially limit the owner's ability to maximize their tax-deductible contributions.

CHAPTER TWO

Introduction to Retirement Plans

Comprehensive retirement strategies play a pivotal role in securing financial stability during one's later years. The notion of retirement planning boasts a profound historical backdrop, particularly within the United States, having undergone substantial evolution to adapt to shifting economic dynamics and demographic demands. Proficiency in these strategies is imperative not only for individual fiscal prosperity but also for bolstering societal economic resilience.

The Essence of Retirement Planning

- **Definition and Purpose:**

A retirement plan constitutes a financial framework crafted to supplant income derived from employment upon retirement. These plans are typically instituted by employers, although self-employed individuals retain the capacity to establish them.

- **Significance:**

Retirement planning transcends mere monetary accumulation; its essence lies in ensuring a resilient and gratifying lifestyle post-retirement. Additionally, it functions as a safeguard against the erosive effects of inflation and potential healthcare expenditures in advanced age.

Types of Retirement Plans

- **Defined Contribution Plans:**

Such plans, exemplified by the 401(k), empower individuals to allocate a portion of their earnings into a retirement fund. The benefits accrued hinge upon the performance of investments. Key attributes encompass employee contributions, tax-deferred growth, and potential employer matching (where applicable).

- **Defined Benefit Plans:**

Conventional pension plans fall into this category. They pledge a predetermined monthly stipend upon retirement, typically contingent on factors such as salary and tenure of service. Primarily, the onus of investment risk lies with the employer.

- **Hybrid Plans:**

Cash Balance Defined Benefit Plan and Profit Share/401k plans combined offer a blend of adaptability and enhanced contribution percentages for proprietors, all while adhering to nondiscrimination testing regulations for employees.

Importance of Retirement Planning

1. **Managing Longevity Risk:**

As life expectancies continue to rise, individuals face the significant challenge of ensuring that their retirement savings outlast their lifespan. This is what's known as longevity risk. It's not just about having enough money for retirement; it's about strategizing to ensure that funds are available for the entirety of one's retirement years. This necessitates careful planning, investment diversification, and potentially exploring options like annuities that provide guaranteed income for life.

2. **Economic and Social Impact:**

Retirement planning isn't just a personal endeavor; it has broader implications for society and the economy. By effectively planning for retirement, individuals can reduce their reliance on government-funded social security programs. This, in turn, helps to alleviate the strain on public resources and contributes to overall economic stability. A populace that is financially secure in retirement is better equipped to contribute to economic growth and stability.

3. **Misconceptions and Lack of Awareness:**

One of the biggest obstacles to effective retirement planning is the prevalence of misconceptions and a general lack of awareness. Many individuals underestimate the amount of money they'll need to maintain their desired lifestyle in retirement. Additionally, there's often a lack of understanding about the impact of factors such as inflation and investment risks on long-term savings. Addressing these misconceptions and enhancing financial literacy are essential components of successful retirement planning efforts.

4. **Navigating Complex Financial Products:**

The landscape of financial products available for retirement planning can be overwhelming and complex. From employer-sponsored retirement plans like 401(k)s to individual retirement accounts (IRAs), there's a myriad of options to consider. Each option comes with its own set of rules, tax implications, and investment choices. Navigating this complexity requires careful consideration of individual goals, risk tolerance, and financial circumstances, often with the guidance of a financial advisor.

5. **Shielding Retirement Assets from Creditors:**

In today's litigious society, protecting retirement assets from creditors is a crucial consideration. Fortunately, there are legal mechanisms in place, such as the Employee Retirement Income Security Act (ERISA), which provides strong protections for retirement savings. Understanding these protections and taking proactive steps to shield assets can provide peace of mind and ensure that retirement funds remain secure, even in the face of potential legal challenges.

CHAPTER THREE

Early 20th Century Defined Benefit Plan Problems

The history and evolution of the Early Defined Benefit (DB) plan to the current Cash Balance Defined Benefit combination plan is a fascinating journey that reflects broader economic trends, changing workforce dynamics, and evolving attitudes toward retirement planning. Initially, traditional Defined Benefit plans were the cornerstone of retirement security, offering employees a predictable and stable income based on years of service and salary history. These plans were highly valued for reliability, providing a guaranteed monthly benefit upon retirement.

However, as the economy transformed and the workforce became more mobile, the limitations of these early DB plans became apparent. The rigidity of traditional DB plans, which favored long-term employees at a single company, did not align well with the increasing prevalence of career changes and the gig economy. This shift necessitated a more flexible approach to retirement planning.

Early Defined Benefit Plans

Defined Benefit plans, in their traditional form, have been a cornerstone of retirement planning since the early 20th century. These plans promise a specific retirement benefit, typically a monthly pension, calculated based on factors such as the employee's salary and years of service. This model provided employees with a sense of security, knowing they would receive a guaranteed income upon retirement. It was particularly reassuring in an era when long-term employment with a single company was the norm.

The reliability of traditional Defined Benefit plans made them an attractive component of employee compensation packages. Employers used these plans to attract and retain talent, offering a stable and predictable retirement income that was directly tied to the employee's tenure and earnings. This structure encouraged long-term loyalty and provided a clear financial incentive for employees to remain with their employers for extended periods.

Characteristics and Problems of Early DB Plans

1. Employer Responsibility: The employer was responsible for managing the plan's investments and ensuring sufficient funds to pay promised benefits. This meant that the burden of investment risk and the obligation to meet future payment commitments fell squarely on the shoulders of the employer. Companies had to carefully manage their pension funds, making strategic investment decisions to grow the assets while also maintaining a sufficient reserve to meet the actuarial calculations of future liabilities.

2. Predictable Income: They provided employees with a predictable, often lifelong, income after retirement. This guaranteed income stream was one of the most appealing features of traditional Defined Benefit plans. Employees could retire with confidence, knowing they would receive a stable monthly pension for the rest of their lives. This predictability was crucial for financial planning, allowing retirees to budget and manage their expenses without the uncertainty of fluctuating income.

3. Popularity in the Industrial Era: Defined Benefit (DB) plans were particularly popular in industries with long-term employees and a stable workforce. During the Industrial Era, many companies valued the stability and loyalty of their workers, and DB plans were a strategic tool to encourage long-term employment. These industries, such as manufacturing, utilities, and large corporations, often had predictable employment patterns and relatively low employee turnover, making DB plans an ideal fit.

4. Problems with Early Defined Benefit (DB) plans, while revolutionary in providing retirement security, presented several challenges for small business owners. These issues stemmed from the inherent design of traditional DB plans, which were more suited to larger organizations with stable, long-term workforces. The specific problems faced by small business owners included:

1. High Costs and Funding Requirements

- **Initial Setup and Maintenance:** Setting up and maintaining a Defined Benefit (DB) plan often involves significant administrative costs, which could be prohibitively expensive for small businesses. The complexity of DB plans required substantial financial and administrative resources. Employers had to establish the plan, which included creating detailed plan documents, setting up funding mechanisms, and ensuring compliance with regulatory requirements.

- **Ongoing Funding Obligations:** Small businesses had to commit to regular, often substantial, contributions to fund the promised benefits, irrespective of the business's financial performance. This commitment required employers to consistently allocate a significant portion of their financial resources to the pension fund, ensuring that the plan remained adequately funded to meet future benefit obligations.

2. Complex Actuarial Calculations and Management

- **Actuarial Risks:** Defined Benefit (DB) plans require actuarial expertise to calculate the funding necessary to meet future obligations. Small businesses typically lack in-house actuarial capabilities, adding to the complexity and cost. Accurately predicting the amount needed to fulfill future pension benefits involves complex calculations and assumptions about factors such as employee life expectancy, salary increases, and retirement ages. These predictions must be regularly updated to reflect changing circumstances and ensure the plan remains adequately funded.

- **Liability Management:** Managing the long-term liabilities associated with Defined Benefit (DB) plans can be challenging, especially for small businesses with limited financial resources. These plans promise employees a specific retirement benefit, typically based on factors such as salary and years of service. This means that employers must ensure they have sufficient assets to cover these future benefit obligations, which can span decades into the future.

3. Inflexibility and Lack of Portability

- **Inflexible Benefit Structures:** Early Defined Benefit (DB) plans were often rigid in their design, offering little flexibility to adjust benefits in response to changing business circumstances. These plans typically provide employees with a predetermined retirement benefit based on factors such as years of service and salary history, with little room for customization or adaptation.
- **Portability Issues:** Traditional Defined Benefit (DB) plans were not portable, meaning employees leaving before a certain tenure would often lose out on significant pension benefits. This lack of

portability posed challenges in a workforce that was beginning to value mobility and career flexibility.

4. Regulatory and Compliance Burdens

- **Regulatory Challenges:** Navigating the complex regulatory environment of Defined Benefit (DB) plans, including compliance with ERISA (Employee Retirement Income Security Act) standards, posed a significant challenge for employers, especially small businesses. ERISA, enacted in 1974, sets forth comprehensive guidelines for the administration and management of employee benefit plans, including pension plans like DB plans.

- **Reporting Requirements:** Defined Benefit (DB) plans required extensive reporting and disclosure, adding to the administrative burden for small businesses. Compliance with regulatory requirements, such as those mandated by ERISA (Employee Retirement Income Security Act), necessitated detailed reporting on various aspects of the plan's administration, funding, and financial status.

Conclusion

While early Defined Benefit plans provided a foundation for retirement security, their structure and requirements often made them impractical and burdensome for small business owners. These challenges paved the way for the development of more flexible and manageable retirement solutions, such as Designer DB Plus®, a Cash Balance Defined Benefit/ profit share/401(k) combination plan, which better aligns with the needs and capacities of small business owners.

The rigid nature of traditional Defined Benefit plans, with their fixed benefit formulas, complex administrative requirements, and significant funding obligations, created hurdles that many small business owners found difficult to overcome. The administrative burden and financial risks associated with these plans could be particularly daunting for small businesses with limited resources and administrative capabilities.

CHAPTER FOUR

Transition to Cash Balance Profit Share/ 401k Combination Plans

Cash Balance plans emerged in the 1980s as a hybrid between traditional Defined Benefits (DB) plans and Defined Contribution (DC) plans. They still classify as DB plans but incorporate elements that resemble DC plans. In a Cash Balance plan, a participant's account receives an annual credit based on salary, age, plus any interest or appreciation of assets.

These plans offer a blend of predictability and flexibility, addressing some of the challenges associated with traditional DB plans while providing benefits that are more transparent and portable. The annual credit in a Cash Balance plan typically consists of a percentage of the participant's salary, which grows each year. An interest credit is applied, which can be either a fixed rate or tied to an external index, such as Treasury bond yields. Assets can be invested in stocks, bonds, ETFs, Treasuries, or any other suitable investments.

The contemporary landscape of retirement planning is witnessing a growing popularity of Modern Hybrid Cash Balance Profit Sharing/401k plans. This trend underscores a significant shift in how both employers and employees approach retirement savings, blending the advantages of traditional pension plans with the flexibility and individual control characteristic of modern financial planning. These hybrid plans are increasingly favored for their ability to cater to diverse financial needs and their adaptability to changing economic conditions or changes to cash flow.

Modern Hybrid Cash Balance Profit Sharing/401(k) plans offer a dynamic combination of features that address the limitations of both traditional Defined Benefit (DB) and Defined Contribution (DC) plans. By integrating the predictable benefits of Cash Balance plans with the customizable contributions of 401(k) plans, these hybrid models provide a comprehensive retirement solution.

Key aspects of this transition include:

- **Changing Workforce Dynamics:**

As workforce mobility increased, shorter tenure at companies made old traditional DB plans less attractive. The modern workforce is characterized by frequent job changes, career shifts, and a desire for flexibility. Employees are less likely to spend their entire careers with a single employer, and this trend has profound implications for retirement planning.

Old Traditional DB plans, which often required long vesting periods and were based on final salary and years of service, became less appealing in this context. Employees who changed jobs frequently would not stay long enough to fully vest their pension benefits, resulting in a significant loss of retirement income.

The lack of portability in old traditional DB plans meant that employees could not easily transfer their accumulated benefits to a new employer's plan, leaving them at a disadvantage compared to those who remained with a single employer for many years.

- **Simplicity and Transparency:**

Cash balance plan investments are typically simpler to comprehend as they provide a transparent account balance. Employer contributions are added to a combined pooled account, eliminating the need for individual, time-consuming investment choices for each employee.

The adoption of Cash Balance Defined Benefit, Profit Share/401k combination plans by small business owners is increasingly recognized as a crucial strategy for achieving significant tax savings while simultaneously amassing the substantial funds necessary to replace a considerable portion of salary in retirement. This need is particularly acute for small business owners who often face unique challenges in preparing for retirement, including variable income streams and the lack of a corporate-style pension plan.

The Imperative for Small Business Owners

Small business owners typically do not have access to the comprehensive retirement plans available in larger corporations. Consequently, they must be more proactive and strategic in their retirement planning. These plans offer the dual benefits of a predictable, defined benefit similar to traditional pensions while allowing for flexibility in contributions, which can be tailored based on business performance. Cash Balance Defined Benefit plans provide a powerful tool in this regard due to several key reasons:

1. **High Contribution Limits:**

Cash Balance plans allow for significantly higher contribution limits compared to traditional 401(k), SEP, Solo 401k, or IRA plans. This feature is particularly beneficial for small business owners who need to catch up on their retirement savings or wish to save larger amounts in a shorter time frame. These tax-deductible contributions can range from $75,000 to $1,000,000 in a single year, depending on age, salary, and other variables.

This substantial contribution potential not only accelerates retirement savings but also offers considerable tax advantages, making Cash Balance plans an attractive option for small business owners seeking to optimize their financial planning and secure a robust retirement fund efficiently.

2. **Tax Efficiency:**

Contributions made to a Cash Balance plan are tax-deductible, providing immediate tax relief. Deductions in the form of reducing gross income are one of the most powerful straightforward deductions a business can make. This benefit is especially advantageous for high-income earners looking to reduce their taxable income. Contributions are taken from the company's gross profit and can significantly reduce flow-through taxation. They also potentially qualify for a 20% QBI (Qualified Business Income) tax deduction. By reducing the taxable income of the business, owners can lower their overall tax burden, thus freeing up more capital for reinvestment or other financial strategies.

If a company has substantial cash flow in good years, instead of taking depreciation tax deductions to reduce taxes, implementing a Designer DB Plus® Plan can be much more beneficial by putting valuable assets in the owners' pockets (a usable asset – for retirement) rather than buying equipment or some other depreciating asset to help reduce taxes.

Additionally, these contributions can help small business owners potentially qualify for the Qualified Business Income (QBI) tax deduction, further enhancing the plan's tax efficiency. The QBI deduction allows eligible businesses to deduct up to 20% of their qualified business income, provided certain conditions are met.

3. Predictable Retirement Income:

These plans offer a defined benefit at retirement, providing a predictable and reliable source of income that can replace a substantial portion of the owner's pre-retirement salary. This stability is particularly valuable for small business owners who might otherwise face uncertainty in their retirement income due to the variability of business performance and personal investments.

By guaranteeing a specific benefit amount based on the participant's salary, age, and years to retirement, Cash Balance plans ensure that retirees have a steady stream of income, mitigating the financial risks associated with market fluctuations and investment returns. This predictable income stream can greatly enhance financial security in retirement, allowing small business owners to plan with confidence and maintain their standard of living.

The structure of Cash Balance plans helps align retirement benefits with pre-retirement earnings, ensuring that the retirement income is sufficient to meet ongoing expenses and financial commitments. This predictability contrasts sharply with the potential variability of Defined Contribution plans, where retirement income depends heavily on individual investment decisions and market conditions.

How do Cash Balance Defined Benefit plans get such high contribution limits?

Cash Balance plans allow for significantly higher contributions than traditional 401(k) plans due to their design as Defined Benefit plans rather than Defined Contribution plans. Here's how they achieve these higher contributions:

1. Defined Benefit Structure:

Cash Balance Plan: This is a type of defined benefit plan where the contribution is determined by an actuarial formula that considers factors like age, salary, and years until retirement. The plan promises a specific benefit at retirement, expressed as a lump sum or an annuity, and the contributions required to fund this benefit can be much higher, especially for older, higher-earning employees.

Solo 401(k) Plan: In contrast, a Solo 401(k) is a defined contribution plan where contributions are limited by annual IRS limits. For 2024, the limit is $69,000 for those under 50 and $76,500 for those 50 and older (including catch-up contributions with combined employer and Employee contributions).

2. Age-Weighted Contributions:

In a Cash Balance plan, older employees closer to retirement can receive much larger contributions because the plan needs to ensure they accumulate sufficient funds by the time they retire. The contribution for a younger employee might be lower since they have more years for the funds to grow.

3. Contribution Limits:

While 401(k) plans have strict contribution limits regardless of salary, Cash Balance plans can allow contributions well into six figures for high earners. The actual limit depends on the actuarial assumptions and the maximum allowable lump sum that can be provided under IRS rules at retirement age.

Example:

Let's consider an example based on the highest recognized salary for a Cash Balance plan.

Highest Recognized Salary: For 2024, the IRS compensation limit is $345,000. *(Note: This salary figure is used solely for plan calculation purposes. It does not restrict eligibility for the plan. Business owners with salaries exceeding this amount can still implement and benefit from the plan.)* Age: Assume the individual is 55 years old, which allows for maximum contributions due to the shorter time to retirement.

In this scenario, the contribution to a Cash Balance plan could be as high as $300,000 to $400,000 annually and potentially more with a double-up. The exact amount depends on the plan's specific design, actuarial assumptions, and how much needs to be funded to achieve the target benefit at retirement.

Cash Balance plans allow for much higher contributions than 401(k) plans because they are designed to provide a specific retirement benefit and calculate the contributions to ensure this benefit can be met. Contributions are exceptionally high for older employees and those earning close to the IRS compensation limit. The plan utilizes a conservative actuarial assumption of approximately 5% for investment returns in its calculations. This conservative approach is designed to mitigate the need for high-risk investment strategies that may be subject to significant market volatility and prolonged recovery periods during economic downturns. The substantial tax-deductible contributions permitted under this plan structure effectively eliminate the necessity for aggressive investment tactics to meet retirement funding objectives. This conservative methodology allows for a more stable and predictable path to achieving retirement goals, reducing the reliance on potentially volatile market performance.

The Cash Balance plan offers a distinct advantage through its provision for substantial tax-deductible contributions, significantly mitigating the reliance on aggressive investment strategies. Unlike traditional 401(k) plans with their comparatively modest contribution limits, Cash Balance plans permit considerably higher contributions, with allowances increasing with the participant's age. This structure is predicated on achieving a predetermined defined benefit at retirement rather than solely depending on market-driven asset accumulation. The plan's design intrinsically accommodates larger contributions for older participants, reflecting the shorter time horizon to retirement and the need to reach the specified benefit level. This approach provides a more controlled and predictable path to retirement funding, reducing exposure to market volatility while maximizing tax-efficient savings.

The constrained contribution limits inherent in 401(k) plans frequently compel participants to pursue elevated returns through higher-risk investment vehicles in an effort to accumulate a substantial retirement portfolio. This approach inevitably exposes retirement savings to increased market volatility, potentially subjecting the participant's nest egg to significant fluctuations, particularly during economic downturns. The consequent dependence on market performance to attain an adequate retirement balance can induce considerable stress for participants, especially in periods of economic instability. This reliance on market-driven growth to bridge the gap between allowable contributions and desired retirement outcomes underscores a fundamental challenge within the 401(k) structure, potentially compromising the financial security and peace of mind of participants as they approach retirement.

The Cash Balance plan, with its elevated contribution limits, facilitates the accumulation of substantially larger sums on a tax-deferred basis annually. This enhanced contribution capacity significantly diminishes the imperative to pursue high-yield, high-risk investment strategies. Consequently, participants have the flexibility to opt for more conservative investment vehicles that inherently carry lower risk profiles. The paradigm shifts from a returns-centric approach to one that prioritizes the confluence of substantial contributions and moderate, consistent investment returns to meet the predetermined defined benefit objective. This reorientation allows for the achievement of retirement goals with markedly reduced exposure to market volatility and associated risks. The resultant framework provides participants with enhanced financial stability and greater peace of mind as the path to retirement becomes less dependent on unpredictable market performance and more reliant on the structured, high-contribution model inherent in the Cash Balance plan design.

The significant tax deductions afforded by Cash Balance plan contributions serve a dual purpose: they substantially reduce current tax liabilities while simultaneously amplifying retirement savings through compounding effects over time. This approach facilitates a more equilibrated retirement planning strategy, shifting the focus from high-risk, high-return pursuits to a model prioritizing financial security and consistent growth. The synergy between tax efficiency and steady accumulation exemplifies a sophisticated approach to retirement planning, aligning long-term financial objectives with a more conservative risk profile.

This version provides a more detailed comparison between Cash Balance plans and 401(k) plans, emphasizing the benefits of higher contributions, reduced risk, and the tax advantages associated with Cash Balance plans.

Maximum Contributions 2024

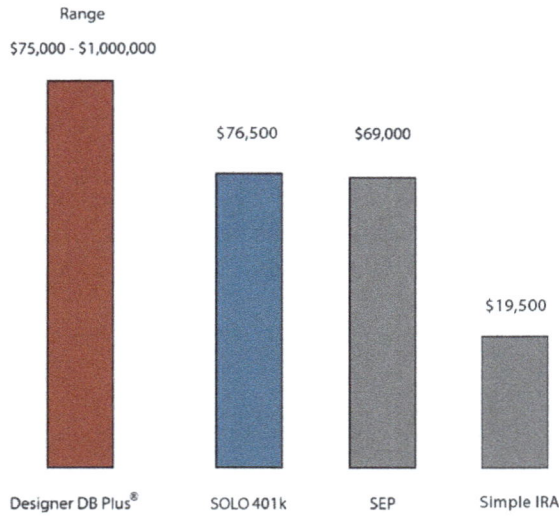

CHAPTER FIVE

21st Century Retirement Planning Solution

The Solution: Designer DB Plus® A Hybrid Cash Balance/ Profit Share/401k and 401h Combination plan

The combination of a Cash Balance Defined Benefit plan, Profit Sharing/401(k), and 401(h) plan offers a compelling solution to these issues by integrating the strengths of multiple retirement and health benefit structures into a comprehensive strategy. This multifaceted approach addresses the diverse needs of small business owners and their employees, ensuring robust financial security and flexibility:

1. **High Contribution Limits:** These plans allow for much higher annual contributions compared to traditional retirement plans, enabling owners

to rapidly accelerate their retirement savings. This feature is particularly advantageous for small business owners who may need to catch up on their retirement savings or who wish to maximize their contributions within a shorter time frame.

By leveraging the high contribution limits of Cash Balance Defined Benefit plans, owners can contribute amounts that far exceed the caps placed on traditional 401(k) or IRA plans. For example, depending on factors such as age, salary, and years until retirement, contributions to a Cash Balance plan can range from $75,000 to $1,000,000 in a single year, depending on the case. This capacity for substantial contributions not only boosts retirement savings quickly but also provides significant tax benefits, as these contributions are tax-deductible.

2. **Tax Advantages:** Contributions to these plans are tax-deductible, providing immediate tax relief and reducing the owner's taxable income. This tax efficiency is particularly beneficial for high-income earners and small business owners who are looking to optimize their financial strategies. By making substantial contributions to Cash Balance Defined Benefit plans, Profit Sharing/401(k) plans, and 401(h) plans, business owners can significantly lower their current tax liabilities.

3. **Flexibility and Control:** The combination of different plan types offers flexibility in terms of investment options and contributions, allowing

business owners to tailor their retirement strategy to their specific needs. This versatility is particularly valuable for small business owners who require adaptable solutions to meet their unique financial situations and goals.

4. **Creditor Protection:** ERISA-covered retirement plans provide strong creditor protection. This means that the assets within these retirement plans are generally safeguarded from creditors in the event of bankruptcy or legal judgments. For small business owners, this protection is crucial, as it ensures that their retirement savings remain secure and untouchable, even in the face of financial difficulties or lawsuits.

5. **Tax Credits**: Tax credits that can help pay for the plan implementation under the Secure Act of 2020. These credits are particularly beneficial for small business owners, making it more affordable to set up and administer retirement plans. Under the Secure Act, businesses can receive a credit of up to $16,500 to cover the costs associated with starting a retirement plan. Secure Act 2.0 increased the ability to receive even larger credits over five years on employer-sponsored plans such as a Designer DB Plus® plan.

Tax-Free Medical Expense Reimbursement Account

Post-Retirement Medical Expense Reimbursement Benefit is the most overlooked benefit in the industry. One of the largest expenses a retiree faces is their health care costs in retirement.

Health Care Costs For Average American Couple Retiring Today

According to a report from RBC Wealth Management, the projected lifetime cost of care for a healthy 65-year-old is $404,253—and that doesn't factor in long-term care costs, which could be as high as $100,000 a year or more.

Under IRC Code Section 401(h), a Post-Retirement Medical Expense Reimbursement Account can be distributed tax-free for post-retirement medical benefits. Employers can create an account and take a 100% deduction, grow the fund's tax-deferred, and then distribute the funds tax-free for post-retirement medical benefits.

A 401(h) account is a specialized medical expense Reimbursement account that can only be added to a Defined Benefit Plan. It's designed to fund health benefits for retired employees (and their spouses and dependents), covering costs associated with sickness, accident, hospitalization, long-term care, and other medical expenses. This account allows for the accumulation of significant funds specifically earmarked for healthcare expenses, ensuring that retirees have the financial resources to manage their medical needs without compromising their overall retirement savings.

By integrating a 401(h) account with a Defined Benefit Plan, employers can offer a comprehensive benefits package that addresses both retirement income and healthcare security. Contributions to a 401(h) account are tax-advantaged, providing immediate tax relief to the business while building a dedicated fund for future medical expenses.

1. **High Cost of Medical Expenses:** A Tax-Free Medical Expense Reimbursement account can currently accumulate up to $632,000 per participant to pay for medical expenses in retirement and take periodic raises to adjust for increased medical costs and inflation. This feature addresses one of the most significant financial concerns for retirees: the rising cost of healthcare. By dedicating a substantial sum specifically to medical expenses, retirees can ensure that they have the necessary funds to cover healthcare costs without depleting their other retirement savings.

2. **Tax Benefits:** Contributions to a 401(h) account are tax-deductible, and earnings in the account grow tax-free. Medical benefits paid from the account are **not taxable** to the retiree as long as they are used for qualified medical expenses. This is a tax trifecta that no retirement plan should be without. The combination of tax-deductible contributions, tax-free growth, and tax-free withdrawals for medical expenses maximizes the financial efficiency of the plan.

For small business owners, this tax advantage means they can significantly reduce their taxable income by contributing to a 401(h) account while also ensuring that their contributions grow without being eroded by taxes.

3. **Retirement-Linked:** A 401(h) account is linked to a defined benefit plan and is meant to provide post-retirement medical reimbursement benefits. It is only available to owners and employees who retire from the company or are considered retired due to permanent disability. The linkage to a defined benefit plan ensures that retirees have a dedicated fund to cover healthcare expenses, including medical, hospitalization, long-term care, and other qualified medical costs.

   By integrating a 401(h) account with a defined benefit plan, employers can offer retirees a comprehensive benefits package that extends beyond traditional retirement benefits. This inclusion enhances the overall attractiveness of the retirement plan and helps businesses attract and retain valuable employees by providing robust post-retirement healthcare coverage.

4. **Funding and Usage:** These accounts are used to reimburse post-retirement medical expenses not covered by insurance or Medicare. This can include insurance premiums, prescriptions, co-pays, dental costs, and long-term care, depending on the plan's provisions.

   By accumulating funds in a 401(h) account, retirees can effectively supplement their existing insurance coverage or Medicare benefits, ensuring that they have the financial resources to manage various medical expenses as they age. This targeted funding approach allows retirees to maintain their health and well-being without relying solely on out-of-pocket expenses or depleting their other retirement savings.

The main advantages include tax-deductible contributions, tax-deferred investment growth, and reimbursement for qualified medical expenses without taxation. The disadvantages include the need for a custom plan document and challenges in plan management.

Retirement Actuarial Services has years of experience with designing custom plans and administering Cash Balance DB Profit Share/401(k) plans, along with 401(h) benefits. This experience ensures that businesses can navigate the complexities associated with these retirement plans effectively.

Example of Medical Expense Reimbursement Benefits	
Acupuncture	Hospitalization Insurance
ADD Counseling and Assistance	Hospital Bills
Air Lift Transportation	Insulin
Alcoholism	Laboratory Fees
Alternative Healthcare	Laetrile by Prescription
Alternative Medicines	Lasik Eye Surgery
Ambulance	Hire Lead Base Paid Removal-Children
Artificial Limbs	with Lead Poisoning
Artificial Teeth	Retirement Home for Medical Care
Assisted Living Facilities	Long Term Care, Nursing Homes
Asthma and Allergy Treatment	Medical Information Plan
Birth Control Pills	Medicines

Braces	Membership Fees for Medical Services,
Braille-Books and Magazines	Hospitalization, Clinical Care, Health
Chiropractors	Maintenance, Health club memberships
Christian Science Practitioners" Fees	Nurses Fees, Nurses Room and Board
Contact Lenses Including Exam Fee	S.S. Tax (Where Paid by Taxpayer)
Co-Pays	Obstetrical Expenses
Cosmetic Surgery (Even Though	Operations (100% of All Costs)
not by a Physician)	Orthopedic Shoes
Cost for Care Outside the United States	Oxygen
Cost of Operations & Related Treatments	Personal Trainers
Counseling	Physical Therapy

Crutches	Physician Fees
Deductibles	Premiums for LTC
Dental Cosmetic Surgery	Preventive care including but not limited to
Dental Fees	Spa Facilities, Usage Fees for Facilities
Dentures	Prosthetics
Dependent Care	Psychiatric Care
Dermatologist Care	Psychologist Fees
Diagnostic Fees	"Seeing-eye" Dog and its Upkeep
Drugs	Specialists and Specialized Treatments
Electrolysis	Specially Equipped Cars
Experimental Care	Special Care Costs for Disabled Dependents

Eyeglasses, Including Examination Fee,	Special Diets
Laser Surgery for Vision Correction	Sterilization Fees
Fees of Practical Nurse	Support Groups
Fees for Healing Services	Surgical Fees
Fees of Chiropractors	Therapy Treatments
Fees for Fitness Programs and Facilities	Transport Expenses for Medical Services
Fees of Licensed Osteopaths	>including Preventative Care
Flu Shots	Tuition at Special School for Handicapped
Hair Transplants	Viagra
Health Insurance Premiums	Vitamins
Hearing Devices and Batteries	Wheelchair
Hospice	Weight Loss Programs
In-Home Care	X-rays

Conclusion

The integration of the Designer DB Plus® plan presents a viable and effective solution to the retirement planning crisis faced by small business owners in America. By allowing for substantial tax-deductible contributions and offering a structured approach to saving, these hybrid plans not only address the immediate need for accelerated retirement savings but also provide a pathway toward financial security and stability in retirement. This strategy is particularly crucial for small business owners, who are often at a disadvantage when it comes to traditional retirement planning avenues.

Small business owners can benefit significantly from the tax advantages inherent in these integrated plans. Contributions made to a Customized Designer DB Plus® plan are tax-deductible, reducing current taxable income and providing immediate financial relief. This tax efficiency allows owners to allocate more resources toward retirement savings while simultaneously lowering their tax liabilities, thereby optimizing their overall financial strategy.

CHAPTER SIX

Why hasn't my tax advisor recommended this to me?

Cash Balance Plans/Profit Share/401k combination plans may not be widely known among individuals or tax advisors for several reasons:

1. **Complexity and Specificity:** Cash Balance Plans are typically more intricate compared to common retirement plans such as 401(k)s SEPs, Solo 401k, or Simple IRAs. They involve actuarial calculations, reporting, and testing requirements. The intricacy and the requirement for specialized knowledge in administering the plan may result in tax advisors' lack of reliable resources in this specialized field, coupled with the lack of educational platforms available to bring tax professionals up

to date on changes annually, which may result in a reluctance to discussing these strategies more frequently.

The complexity of these plans arises from the need to determine annual contribution credits and interest credits, which requires a deep understanding of actuarial science. Additionally, the funding requirements for Cash Balance Plans are more stringent, requiring regular evaluations to ensure that the plan is adequately funded to meet future benefit obligations. This is where working with a knowledgeable third-party administrator like Retirement Actuarial Services necessitates ongoing collaboration with actuaries and compliance with numerous regulatory standards, which can be daunting for those not well-versed in such specifics.

Furthermore, the administrative responsibilities associated with Cash Balance Plans/Profit Share/401k plans are substantial. Employers must ensure accurate record-keeping, compliance with ERISA guidelines, and timely contribution funding, all of which add layers of complexity compared to more simplified retirement plans.

2. **Target Demographic:** While these plans can be advantageous for any sole proprietor, S corp, Partnership, or 1099 contractor business owner 21-75 years of age seeking to minimize tax obligations and establish a retirement plan, some tax advisors may be more familiar with the

previous DB Plans that necessitated business owners to meet specific demographic criteria and maintain a stable cash flow.

Traditional Defined Benefit (DB) Plans often require business owners to have a relatively homogenous workforce and consistent revenue streams to manage long-term funding commitments effectively. These plans demanded regular, predictable contributions to ensure the promised benefits could be met, which could be challenging for businesses with fluctuating incomes or diverse employee demographics.

As a result, tax advisors who are accustomed to these older DB Plans may not be as familiar with the more flexible structure of Cash Balance/Profit Share/401k Combination plans. These modern plans offer greater adaptability to varying business conditions and do not impose the same stringent demographic or cash flow requirements. This flexibility makes Cash Balance Plans particularly suitable for a wider range of businesses, including those with more volatile earnings or diverse employee bases.

3. **Lack of Awareness or Expertise:** Because of the insufficient and inconsistent education regarding these strategies and the constant changes in laws during the last couple of decades, tax advisors are facing challenges in staying well-informed about all the intricate details involved. Consequently, they often suggest simpler strategies that they believe will help fulfill the client's requirements.

The frequent changes in retirement plan regulations and tax laws make it difficult for tax advisors to stay updated on the latest developments, especially given the complexity of Cash Balance Plans and similar hybrid retirement strategies. These plans require a deep understanding of both actuarial principles and regulatory compliance, which necessitates continuous education and specialized training.

Many tax advisors may not have access to comprehensive and consistent educational resources that adequately cover these advanced retirement planning options. The sporadic nature of educational opportunities and the rapid pace of legislative changes can lead to gaps in knowledge, making it challenging for advisors to confidently recommend and implement these sophisticated plans.

4. **Resources and ongoing Education:** The implementation and maintenance of these plans typically require a substantial amount of time and in-depth knowledge, which can be overwhelming for tax advisors. As a result, many tax advisors are now partnering with third-party administrators to ensure the plan is properly implemented.

The complexity of Cash Balance Plans, including the need for precise actuarial calculations, compliance with intricate regulations, and continuous plan management, demands significant expertise and resources. Tax advisors who already juggle multiple clients' needs and stay abreast of evolving tax laws may find the additional burden of managing these specialized plans daunting.

To address this challenge, many tax advisors collaborate with third-party administrators (TPAs). These professionals specialize in the design, implementation, and administration of complex retirement plans, including Cash Balance Plans. By leveraging the expertise of a Third-Party Administrator (TPA), tax advisors and small business owners can ensure that retirement plans are set up correctly, comply with all legal requirements, and operate smoothly over time in a cost-effective manner.

CHAPTER SEVEN

Additional Benefits of the Designer DB Plus® Plan

The Designer DB Plus® plan offers various benefits, including the option to incorporate tax-deductible life insurance into your retirement strategy. While this option may not be suitable for everyone, understanding the pros and cons based on your specific situation is essential. If you choose to include a life insurance policy within the plan, it must be specifically structured to be effective. Several factors must be considered, such as surrender charges, premium structure, duration, and product type. Additionally, regulations limit how much death benefit can be purchased within the plan. A flexible premium policy is preferable to adjust to varying contributions annually. Consulting with an advisor experienced in life insurance and Defined Benefit plans is crucial.

How Tax-Deductible Life Insurance Works in the Designer DB Plus® Plan:

1. Integration with Retirement Contributions:

The Designer DB Plus® plan allows life insurance to be integrated into the business's retirement contributions. A portion of the contributions normally allocated to the retirement fund can be used to purchase a life insurance policy. The premiums paid for this life insurance are tax-deductible, just like the contributions to the retirement plan itself.

2. Protection and Wealth Transfer:

Including life insurance within the Designer DB Plus® plan provides death benefit protection and facilitates efficient wealth transfer. The life insurance proceeds can be tax-free to the beneficiaries upon the policyholder's death, providing significant financial security to loved ones.

3. Cash Value Accumulation:

Depending on the type of life insurance policy chosen (e.g., whole life or Indexed Universal Life), the policy may build cash value over time. This cash value grows tax-deferred within the plan. Once the policy is terminated or surrendered, the cash value becomes part of the plan's assets, and the insurance coverage ceases. Advanced strategies, such as buying the policy out of the plan at fair market value, exist for those who wish to maintain coverage, but this involves complex rules to avoid prohibited transactions.

4. **Enhanced Tax Efficiency:**

By making life insurance premiums tax-deductible, the Designer DB Plus® plan reduces the overall tax burden for the business. This is particularly advantageous for high-income business owners seeking to shelter income from taxes while securing their family's financial future.

5. **Customizable to Individual Needs:**

The Designer DB Plus® plan is highly customizable, allowing business owners to tailor the life insurance component to their specific needs and financial goals within certain guidelines. Whether focusing on maximizing retirement income for a spouse in the event of early death or ensuring business continuity, the life insurance element can be adjusted to align with these objectives.

In summary, the Designer DB Plus® plan's provision for tax-deductible life insurance may enhance its overall benefits by offering tax-efficient ways to protect and transfer wealth, build additional savings, and ensure a secure financial future for the business owner and their beneficiaries.

Tax Reduction Strategy for Business Sale

The Designer DB Plus® plan offers a powerful strategy for business owners looking to reduce taxes upon the sale of their business while facilitating a smooth and financially feasible succession plan for family members.

1. **Maximized Retirement Contributions:**

One of the key features of the Designer DB Plus® plan is the ability to make substantial contributions to a Cash Balance Defined Benefit plan, significantly reducing the business's taxable income in the years leading up to the sale. By funding the plan aggressively, the business owner can lower their overall tax liability, keep more wealth within the plan, and reduce the immediate tax burden from business operations.

2. **Deferred Taxation on Pension Distributions:**

The funds accumulated in the Designer DB Plus® plan are not taxed until they are withdrawn, typically during retirement when the owner may be in a lower tax bracket. This deferral provides a significant tax advantage, as the owner can potentially reduce their overall tax liability by strategically timing the distribution of these funds.

Facilitating Succession Planning

1. **Fully Funded Pension Plan:**

With the Designer DB Plus® plan, the business owner can ensure that their retirement is fully funded independently of the business sale proceeds. This financial security allows the owner to be more flexible in structuring the sale of the business to a family member who may not be in a financial position to pay the full market value upfront.

2. **Structured Buy-Out Options:**

The plan can help facilitate structured buy-out arrangements, allowing the family member to gradually take over ownership without requiring a large lump-sum payment. With a fully funded pension, the owner is less likely to need a significant lump-sum sale to retire. This is particularly advantageous if the family member lacks the financial resources to purchase the company outright.

3. **Business Continuity:**

The Designer DB Plus® plan supports business continuity within the family by reducing the financial strain on the next generation. With the owner's retirement needs secured through a fully funded pension, there is less pressure to sell the business to an outside party. This makes it easier for a family member to step in, maintain operations, and continue the business legacy.

4. **Estate Planning Benefits:**

The plan can also be integrated with broader estate planning strategies. By ensuring the business owner's retirement is secured through the Designer DB Plus® plan, it may be possible to transfer the business to a family member with reduced estate tax implications. This can be achieved through gifting strategies, family-limited partnerships, or other techniques designed to minimize estate taxes while ensuring the business remains in the family.

5. **Flexibility in Succession Timing:**

With the financial pressure alleviated by the Designer DB Plus® plan, the business owner has the flexibility to plan for succession at the most opportune time, both for themselves and the family member taking over. This flexibility can lead to a more successful transition, allowing the successor to be properly prepared and the business to be transferred during favorable market conditions.

If the owner depends on selling the business to retire, they may be shocked by the amount of taxes owed, which could leave them short of the needed funds to retire as planned. The Designer DB Plus® plan can help mitigate the tax liability by funding the pension plan ahead of the sale.

The Designer DB Plus® plan offers a comprehensive strategy that not only reduces taxes upon the sale of a business but also facilitates a smooth and financially viable succession plan. By securing the owner's retirement through a fully funded pension, the plan provides the financial flexibility needed to transfer the business to a family member, even if they are not in a position to purchase the business outright. This approach ensures that the business can remain in the family, providing continuity and preserving the legacy the owner has built over the years.

CHAPTER EIGHT

Key Dates for Proactive Tax Planning with a Custom Designer DB Plus® Plan

As a small business owner, you're aware of the importance of planning. Every decision you make impacts not only the success of your business but also your financial future. One powerful tool at your disposal is proactive tax planning with a custom Designer DB Plus® plan. To maximize the benefits of this strategy, understanding the key dates and deadlines is crucial. This chapter outlines the important dates you need to consider to ensure that your tax planning is effective and that your plan is tailored to meet your specific needs.

Understanding the Timeline: Why Timing Matters

A Designer DB Plus® plan offers significant flexibility, allowing you to make contributions that reduce your taxable income. However, the timing of these contributions is critical. By strategically choosing when to set up and contribute to your plan, you can optimize your tax savings while aligning your retirement goals with the financial performance of your business.

One unique advantage of a Designer DB Plus® plan is that it can be established and funded after the fiscal year closes but before the tax filing deadline (including extensions). This flexibility provides the opportunity to assess your business's financial performance over most of the year before committing to contributions.

Important Dates to Consider

Year-End (December 31) Assessment and Planning:

As the calendar year comes to a close, it's important to review your business's financial performance. Although the plan doesn't need to be established by this date, having a preliminary idea of your financial standing will help you make informed decisions when it's time to set up your plan.

Tax Filing Deadline (March 15th/April 15th) Initial Deadline for Contributions:

For most small business owners, March 15/April 15 marks the initial tax filing deadline, depending on how your business is structured for tax purposes. If you haven't filed for an extension, this is your last chance to establish your Designer DB Plus® plan and make contributions that will count toward the previous tax year. Many small business owners, however, choose to file for an extension, giving themselves more time to finalize their tax strategy.

Final Deadline for Contributions (September 15th/October 15th) Extended Deadline:

Filing an extension extends your tax filing deadline to either September 15 or October 15, depending on your business structure. This extension gives you an additional six months to monitor your business's financial performance and decide how much to contribute to your Designer DB Plus® plan. By September 15, you must have your plan in place and your contributions credited if you want them to count for the prior tax year.

Mid-Year Review (March-May) Mid-Year Strategy Session:

Around the end of the 1st quarter through the midpoint of the year, it's beneficial to conduct a review of your business's financials and projections. This review allows you to adjust your strategy as needed and prepares you to make more informed decisions regarding your Designer DB Plus® plan contributions before the September 15 deadline.

Plan Setup Deadline (Before September 15) Customization and Finalization:

By this time, you should work closely with your financial advisor or tax professional, and plan administrator to tailor the Designer DB Plus® plan to your specific needs. This involves finalizing the structure of the plan, determining contribution amounts, and ensuring all paperwork is completed. Remember, the plan must be set up and credited before the September 15 deadline if you're filing on an extension.

Strategic Advantages of Filing an Extension

Filing an extension is common among small business owners for a good reason. The additional time allows you to gain a clearer picture of your financial standing, which is crucial when making significant decisions like contributions to a Designer DB Plus® plan. Here's why this can be advantageous:

Extended Time for Analysis: Extending your filing deadline gives you approximately eight and a half months into the new year to evaluate your business's revenue, expenses, and overall performance. This extended period allows for a more accurate forecast and better decision-making regarding your retirement plan contributions. Proper planning with your tax professional is always suggested to fully understand the pros and cons of filing an extension for your business.

Flexibility in Contribution Amounts: The ability to wait until September to decide on contributions provides significant flexibility. You can adjust contributions based on your actual revenue and profit margins, ensuring that your tax strategy is optimized without straining your cash flow.

Maximizing Tax Deductions: By carefully timing your contributions, you can potentially lower your taxable income for the previous year, reducing your overall tax liability. This is especially valuable in high-income years when a larger deduction could significantly impact your tax obligations.

A Collaborative Team Approach

Implementing a Designer DB Plus® plan is not something you do alone. The most effective plans result from a collaborative effort between you and your professional advisors. Your CPA, financial advisor, and one of our plan specialists at Retirement Actuarial Services will work together to make this plan easy to implement and tailor it to your needs.

CPA/Tax Advisor: Your CPA or tax advisor will provide insights into your business's financial performance and tax situation. They will help determine any necessary changes to your business structure and calculate how much of your contribution will affect your final tax liability.

Financial Advisor: Your financial advisor will assist in integrating the Designer DB Plus® plan into your broader retirement and investment goals. They will ensure that the investments are suitable for this type of plan, meet the fiduciary standard, and align with the plan's funding and investment return goals.

Plan Specialist at Retirement Actuarial Services: Our plan designers are specialists in the intricacies of qualified plans like the Designer DB Plus®. They will handle the technical aspects of setting up plan documents, testing, reporting, and administering the plan, ensuring compliance with IRS and DOL regulations and customization to meet your unique needs.

By leveraging this team's expertise, you can confidently implement a Designer DB Plus® plan that maximizes your tax savings and secures your financial future. The collaborative approach ensures that all aspects of the plan are considered and the process is streamlined and stress-free for you.

Proactive Planning: The Key to Success

Proactive tax planning is essential for small business owners looking to optimize their financial outcomes. By understanding the critical dates and deadlines associated with the Designer DB Plus® plan, you can take full advantage of the opportunities available to you. Remember, the goal is not just to reduce your tax liability but to build a solid foundation for your retirement so you can confidently retire.

Working closely with your financial advisor, CPA/tax advisor, and our team at Retirement Actuarial Services and keeping these dates in mind will ensure that your tax planning is strategic and effective. The flexibility provided by the Designer DB Plus® plan is a powerful tool in your financial arsenal—use it wisely to secure your financial future.

Let's Look at Some More Cases That We Have Implemented:

Sole Prop Opens Designer DB Plus®

CASE: Chad, age 53, is married. He is a successful real estate agent with no employees. Chad has a net profit of $500,000 (after paying self-employment tax).

GOAL: Chad wants to retain more of his earnings, pay lower taxes, secure his retirement savings, and prepare for the high cost of health and medical care in retirement

SOLUTION: Designer DB Plus® Defined Benefit Combo Plan

DEDUCTION: As an owner of a pass-through entity, he may qualify for a tax deduction under (Section 199A) of up to 20% of his Qualified Business Income if his Income is below the $340, 1 oo threshold for married couples.

Designer DB Plus® Plan

Net Profit after Expenses:	$500,000
Plan Contribution	$262,000
Qualified Business Income:	$238,000
Pass-through Deduction:	$47,600
Taxable Income:	$190,400

Results: $262,000 Retirement Savings First Year
$129,304 Tax Savings and Deferral*

* Tax savings compared to no Plan and (Section 199A) OBI deduction. Auumos estimated 37% tax rates. RAS does not provide tax advice. This example is based on specific assumptions and is used for illustrative purposes only.

*Please consult your tax advisor; RAS does not provide tax advice.

Endodontist Practice with 10 Employees opens DESIGNER DB PLUS®

CASE: Dr. Smiley is 49 years old, married, and the owner of a thriving Endodontist practice with ten employees. They file as a Professional Corporation. He nets approximately $1.5M after expenses.

GOAL: Reduce his personal taxes, accelerate his retirement savings to maintain his lifestyle, create tax-free postretirement savings for health & medical care high costs in retirement.

SOLUTION: Designer DB Plus® Defined Benefit Combo Plan

DEDUCTION: This Profession may not qualify for Qualified Business Income Deduction (Section 199A) additional 20% of his Qualified Business Income.

Designer DB Plus® Plan

Net Profit after Expenses:	$1,470,000
Plan Contribution	$1,162,952
Qualified Business Income:	$307,048
QBI Pass-through Deduction: Taxable	0
Income:	$307,048

Results: Percentage to Owner 98%
$1,139,693 Retirement Savings First Year
$470,208 Tax Savings and Deferral*

* Tax savings, compared to no Plan, assumes an estimated 37% tax rate. RAS does not provide tax advice. This example is based on specific assumptions and is used for illustrative purposes only.

*Please consult your tax advisor; RAS does not provide Tax advice.

Construction Company with 30 Employees opens DESIGNER DB PLUS®

CASE: Bill is 61 years old, married, and owns a construction company with thirty employees. They file as an S Corp. He nets approximately $797,000 after expenses.

GOAL: Bill wants to save on taxes, provide employee benefits while controlling costs, and ensure he has enough retirement savings to maintain his lifestyle while simultaneously creating tax-free money for the high cost of Health and Medical expenses in retirement.

SOLUTION: Designer DB Plus® Defined Benefit Combo plan

DEDUCTION: This Profession may not qualify for Qualified Business Income Deduction (Section 199A) additional 20% of his Qualified Business Income.

Designer DB Plus® Plan

Net Profit after Expenses:	$797,471
Plan Contribution:	$561,627
Qualified Business Income:	$235,844
QBI Pass-through Deduction:	-$47,169
Taxable Income:	$188,675

Results: Percentage to Owner 94%
$526,137 Retirement Savings First Year
$249,782 Tax Savings and Deferral*

* Tax savings, compared to no Plan, assumes an estimated 37% tax rate. RAS does not provide tax advice. This example is based on specific assumptions and is used for illustrative purposes only.

*Please consult your tax advisor; RAS does not provide Tax advice.

It is recommended that you explore your options for proactive tax planning and retirement plans before implementing 401k, SEPs, Solo 401k, or Simple IRA. Implementing the wrong plan can be costly. We are available to discuss which plans may be appropriate for you.

If your tax advisor is unfamiliar with these plans, we are available to discuss these types of plans and we provide a complimentary 1-hour CPE course for tax advisors interested in enhancing their knowledge in this field of tax and financial planning. Our course is certified by the National Association of State Boards of Accountancy (NASBA).

Retirement Actuarial Services LLC is registered with the National Association of State Boards of Accountancy (NASBA) as a sponsor of continuing professional education on the National Registry of CPE Sponsors. State boards of accountancy have final authority on the acceptance of individual courses for CPE credit. Complaints regarding registered sponsors may be submitted to the National Registry of CPE Sponsors through its website: www.NASBARegistry.org.

Contact us

Phone: 800.297.4987

Email: admin@rasvcs.com

Web: www.retirementactuarialservices.com

Request Free Proposal

https://retirementactuarialservices.com/proposal-request/

To request a time for a complimentary 1-hour CPE Course via Webinar, please email admin@rasvcs.com or call 800.297.4987.

Our Partners

www.ingramcontent.com/pod-product-compliance
Lightning Source LLC
LaVergne TN
LVHW020145101225
827394LV00015BA/1423